The
Ultimate
Business Owner
Plan

*How To Have The Business And
The Life You Have Always Dreamed Of*

with
Steve Beatty

Here's What's Inside...

5   **Introduction**

7   **The Ultimate Business Owner Plan!**

7   Why More Business Owners Don't Have a Business Plan or Strategy...

9   Focus on the Journey, Not Just the Destination...

10   **How Personal Development Applied to Your Business Can Change What's Possible...**

12   **Your Business Is a Vehicle to Reach Your Life Goals...**

13   **The Ultimate Business Owner Plan Works no Matter Where You Are in Your Business...**

14   **The Ultimate Business Owner Plan Creates a Business Which Supports the Life You Want to Enjoy...**

20   **The Framework for Your Ultimate Business Plan...**

23   **The Context...**

23   **Tax Minimization...**

24 The Threats Every Business Owner Needs to be Aware of...

30 The Building Blocks of The Ultimate Business Owner Plan...

31 There Are Many Reasons to Have an Exit Plan in Place.....

33 Estate Planning...

36 Essential Financial Planning...

38 Retirement Income Plan...

39 Key Employee Incentive/Retention Plan...

41 Legacy Plan...

42 Successful People Do What Unsuccessful Are Unwilling to Do...

44 Here's Exactly How to Get Your Ultimate Business Owner Plan Started...

46 Author Bio

48 Here Is How to Get Your Ultimate Business Owner Plan Designed and in Place...

Introduction

March 2014
Las Vegas, NV

One of the things people often ask
me is how do some business owners
seem to have it all, and others are struggling to get by
year after year?

This book is a result of the answer to that question. I
wanted to show business owners the model I've been
using successfully with my clients for the last 25
years to create the businesses and lives of their
dreams.

What follows is the transcript where I walk you
through the elements to creating a business that fuels
the life of your dreams. It starts with a vision of the
life you aspire to. Then it becomes using the right
strategies to use to grow, protect and ultimately
enjoy the VALUE of the greatest asset you will ever
own, YOUR BUSINESS.

I hope this book educates you, inspires you and helps
change your way of thinking about how to approach
your business not just as a source of income, but as a
way to help you reach all of your goals in life.

Regards,

Steve Beatty

The Ultimate Business Owner Plan!

Susan: Good afternoon, this is Susan Austin and with me today is Steve Beatty from Las Vegas, Nevada. Welcome Steve.

Steve: Thank you Susan, great to be here.

Why More Business Owners Don't Have a Business Plan or Strategy…

Susan: We are going to talk about The Ultimate Business Owner Plan. Do you find most business owners don't have a plan in place Steve?

Steve: If you go look at Stephen Covey's book, <u>First Things First,</u> he talks about things that are important and things which are not important and things which are urgent and not urgent. Business Planning falls in the important category certainly. Most business owners recognize they should do more planning, but because of their busy lives it falls into the non-urgent category. It's not critical today that I plan my future and think about what it is that I'm trying to achieve with my business and my life. As a result, things get pushed to the back burner.

I can say, "Yeah, I'll get to that tomorrow," and tomorrow becomes next month, which becomes next year which becomes next decade, which become "where did my life go?" I think so many business owners live in the important, urgent quadrant of the matrix. They're busy putting out fires, or, to use <u>The E-Myth</u> author Michael Gerber's phrase, they're working in their business, "doing it, doing it, doing it." They are dealing with customer problems, selling stuff, handling employee problems and so forth. They never carve out the time to really think about, "Why am I doing this?"

I think this is true for most business owners. There is always something more pressing to do. There might be other business owners who have simply never thought about it. They never really had the mindset or paradigm to believe I can create whatever I want with my business. My business should be a vehicle to help me get what I want out of life as opposed to just building a business and whatever happens, happens and being completely accidental about it. No one has honestly had this larger discussion with them.

What I'm suggesting is they can be completely intentional about their lives and their businesses. I ask my clients often, "If you could waive a magic wand and create any life you want, what would you create?" And to take it one step further, if you are going to create that life, how could your business be a vehicle to help you get that life? And from there, what would your business have to look like to be that vehicle? I don't think many people stop and do that, at least not in my experience. A lot of the business owners I meet never thought it's possible.

Susan: You're right. I think when we first start a business; we're not looking 20 years down the road. We're all excited about the product we bring to the market and the customers we're going to serve and the people we need to run the organization. You're suggesting before we launch full speed ahead with our business maybe we should stop and figure out the bigger game the business can play in our life and look at things from that angle rather than just build the business and hope it all works out in the end.

Focus on the Journey, *Not* Just the Destination...

Steve: Yes, exactly. I see this process as more of a journey than a destination. I see it as, whether it's today, tomorrow, or 30 years from now, my business can help me get what I want out of life. It's not just money. My business can give me satisfaction. My business can make a difference in the community. My business can fulfill a lot of my needs for relationships with people, my emotional needs, and obviously my financial needs. If I am clear on what those are, I can design my business in a way that it fulfills a lot of those needs. It helps me, again, live the life I want beyond just having a business.

None of us know how long we're going to be on this Earth. Thinking only about 30 years from now when the business reaches a certain point, we miss the boat in my opinion. Too many people plan for retirement and plan to spend their golden years enjoying themselves. They work themselves to the bone during their working career. They get to the end of their career and then never have golden years to enjoy because they're dead or exhausted from working so hard. Why not find a way to enjoy the ride and make it about the journey, and not just about the destination?

Is it important to plan for the future? Absolutely, it is. Should you have an eye on the future? Yes, but you should have one eye on today as well. One way to do that is to set benchmarks. What are some of the benchmarks that I can work towards to help me get to my ultimate goal that would be a great ride along the way? Then, they can have both. They can have a great destination and they can have a great journey.

How Personal Development Applied to Your Business Can Change What's Possible...

Susan: Interesting. What's preventing someone from approaching their business more holistically if you will?

Steve: I think people often see their business life and their personal life as two separate functions. There isn't a separation though between our business and our lives. Our business is a part of our lives. In fact, we probably spend more time with our business than we do anything else. In my experience, people just don't have an awareness of planning out their life like this, let alone their business.

Susan: That is certainly true.

Steve: Most people just wake up and go through the day and are victims to circumstances. It's critical to really plan out what would I like my life to look like. What are the next ten years going to look like? What is the next year going to look like? What's the next quarter going to look like? What is the next week going to look like? What's the next day going to look like?

Plan it out strategically and then do your best to execute it. It's not about being perfect and having to be regimented, and schedule yourself out so rigidly that you don't have time for anything else. If you don't plan on where you're going, how are you ever going to get there?

I think not enough people have the personal development tools to really create the life that they want. Many people aren't taught that they are empowered to make choices and not be a victim of what happens. Or even if they have done some personal development work, they don't connect it with business. They don't realize what an amazing opportunity a business owner has for creating the life they want. Anything they want. It doesn't have to be a certain way. It doesn't have to be how a business school tells us it "should" be. It doesn't have to be how their dad built his business. It doesn't have to be how my friends set up their businesses.

You can really find a way to create a business that fulfills all of your life goals. There are plenty of examples all around us of people who are doing it. It's just somehow people don't think it could work for them as well.

Your Business Is a Vehicle to Reach Your Life Goals...

Susan: I love what you said. Maybe they've been exposed to some personal development along the way, but they don't think to apply it to their business because the business seems separate from their personal life. You're saying, let's stop and design the life you want and then see how the business can support that outcome and not the other way around.

Steve: Let me clarify - it's the framework for what we're doing. I wish I could take ownership for this. The concept is in <u>The E Myth</u> by Michael Gerber. He wrote that book in the mid-80s. Michael Gerber was a personal mentor of mine back in the 90s. I've worked with him and have been using his concepts for years now, so I can't take ownership of it. But I embrace them and I still champion them with my clients.

The Ultimate Business Owner Plan embraces those concepts with some traditional financial planning to help people ultimately do three things: grow, protect and ultimately enjoy the value of the greatest asset anyone could ever own which is a business. There is no better asset anyone could ever own. A business can be the best financial asset that anyone ever owns without question. But it can be so, so much more.

We see those examples all the time of how business fuels an amazing life of significance like Richard Branson or Bill Gates in the last several years using his wealth to create a foundation that is changing the world. Those two may seem like impossible figures to emulate. But we can create the same thing in our own way. We too can use our business to create the lifestyle that we desire. Imagine the significance that we can create through our businesses, the impact that we could have on our customers and on our employees, and on the community through our business. It's unparalleled.

Thinking of my business and my life in those terms really makes it exciting to me to be a business owner. And I am blessed to work with people to help them unleash the power of that business as a vehicle to create the life they want.

The Ultimate Business Owner Plan Works no Matter Where You Are in Your Business...

Susan: How do you start working with someone? If someone already has a business, but they didn't know to do this 30 years ago when they started out can they still use The Ultimate Business Plan?

Steve: Yes. While it would be ideal to start with someone just opening a business and start this process then, it's almost a fairytale to think someone is going to be able to do that. They don't have enough time in the trenches. They just jump in and start doing their business because that is all they know to do. They do what they see other business owners doing. No one educates them to begin with the end in mind. I think it takes someone that has a few years of battle scars to be able to appreciate how important this process is.

In our business, we always meet someone where they're at. Where you are now is point A. It's the starting point for the rest of your life. The question is where do you imagine point B is? Tell us about where it is that you'd like to go. Again, if you could wave a magic wand and create whatever you want, what would you want to create with your life? And then how can the business help you get there?

Paint a picture of your ideal life. Paint a picture of your ideal business. Then let us show you how we can support you in getting from wherever you're at now towards your ideals. Will you get there immediately? Probably not, but the journey is going to be a heck of a lot better and get you a lot closer to where you want to go than if you just randomly go through life and don't really have a particular target you're shooting for.

The Ultimate Business Owner Plan Creates a Business Which Supports the Life You Want to Enjoy...

Susan: If they do have targets, they are often things like sales goals or income goals. Maybe they assume, if I hit my sales goal, I'll hit my income goal, therefore, I'll have a better life as a result?

Steve: Sales goals are great. But what if there is real meaning attached to those sales goals? Because I hit my sales goals, I've now got enough profit that I can buy a sailboat that my wife and I have always wanted to have to be able to sail from here to Hawaii. with the kids.

Wouldn't that have more meaning? Wouldn't you have more drive towards reaching those sales goals? Wouldn't you find more satisfaction in them than in just hitting the goals just for money's sake? Because I hit my sales goals, I can now make a $25,000 donation to my favorite charity and make a big impact there.

It's different for each person but the framework, the context and the building blocks are the same for every owner to create The Ultimate Business Owner Plan. The Ultimate Business Owner Plan is a proven, step-by-step method for creating a business--AND the financial framework around it--that supports the life I want to enjoy.

Susan: Can you share an exercise with us to help illustrate this?

Steve: Yes. The exercise below provides a good start at looking at where someone is at this moment and has them take a look to where they want to go. Find a quiet spot and answer the following questions for your life and business.

Describe your current personal life: Your lifestyle, your family, your friends. What do you like to spend your time doing outside of work?

_____

_____

_____

_____

Describe your current business life: How did you get started? Why did you choose the business you are in? How would you describe your business successes and challenges? What do you like and don't like about owning your business?

_____

_____

_____

_____

Now, describe where you want to go with your life and business. Don't put any brakes on this process. Dream Big. Your life is worth a bigger dream.

_____

_____

_____

_____

Define your Ultimate Personal Life: Without limits or obstacles - How would you define your Ultimate personal life?

_____

_____

_____

_____

Define your Ultimate Business: Without limits or obstacles - How would you define your Ultimate Business?

_____

_____

_____

_____

Say we are standing together 5 years from now. What would have had to have happened during these past 5 years for you to feel extremely happy with the progress you have made towards your Ultimate Personal Life and Ultimate Business?

_____

_____

_____

_____

Ultimate Life Happenings:

1.

2.

3.

4.

5.

Ultimate Business Happenings:

1.

2.

3.

4.

5.

If you were creating an Action Plan towards your Ultimate Personal Life and Ultimate Business, what actual first steps would be essential to get started - now?

1.

2.

3.

4.

5.

Steve: This exercise is helpful in highlighting the greater goal and vision that maybe hasn't been articulated—or maybe even imagined before. This is the "why" to get up every day and build the business. It's very powerful to complete.

Susan: Especially if someone hasn't looked at this before. It's going to be different for every business owner as well.

The Framework for Your Ultimate Business Plan...

Steve: The answers to the exercises then become the framework for their Ultimate Business Owner Plan.

Susan: Very good. Let's dig into what's in The Ultimate Business Plan!

Steve: We start by talking about building the financial framework. Let's be real, money is the fuel to drive the engine of what most of us want to get out of life. I am sure we all realize money isn't everything. I would bet that many of the goals created in the exercise were about making a difference and having wonderful relationships with friends and family. We then aren't making money for money's sake but money helps enhance the goals the client defines.

Having a great vacation with your spouse and your kids costs money. Could we have a picnic which costs almost nothing and have a great time with them? Absolutely. But I think we all could agree that having money to be able to fuel some of the big goals we have is an important thing.

We talk about this concept of the business and your financial life and how the business is a vehicle to achieve your life goals. We do things differently than most. Instead of financial planning just for the sake of financial planning, we approach financial planning that is tied into your particular life goals. As you'll see there are three parts of what we want to help you do with your business: 1. We want to help you be able to grow the value of your business; 2. We want to help you protect the value of your business; 3. We want to help you ultimately enjoy the value of your business.

We developed a picture of what The Ultimate Business Owner Plan looks like from a financial perspective.

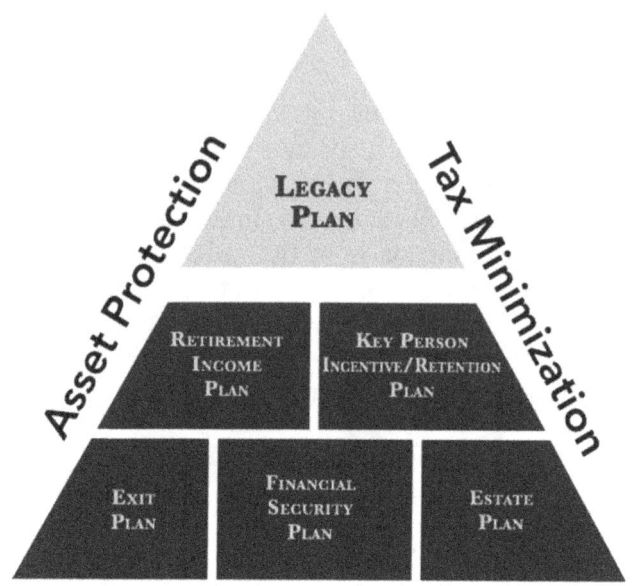

Income Protection

The pyramid is the strongest structure ever created. Many have used it as a metaphor for constructing a strong structure. We add what we know to be the building blocks to building The Ultimate Business Owner Plan: Cornerstones of the Estate Plan and Exit Plan; foundation finished with a Financial Security Plan. As the business and business owner matures, a Retirement Income Plan and Key Person Incentive/Retention Plan must be in place. Ultimately, at maturity the Ultimate Business Owner thinks about his or her Legacy Plan. This is all done in the context of Tax Minimization, Asset Protection and Income Protection.

Building The Ultimate Business Owner Plan and thinking about it in terms of a pyramid is where we start. We look at where someone's at and we work on putting all the building blocks into place...at a pace that is comfortable for the client. It might take years. Each client is different. Each has different goals. That pyramid is the framework for every Ultimate Business Owner Plan. Putting those blocks into place all to reach the goal of living the life you want to live is The Ultimate Business Owner Plan.

The Context...

Around the outside is what we call the context. People don't always key in to what the context is. Think of a jar with a bunch of jellybeans inside. The jellybeans are all the stuff of your business. The jar is the context, it's what keeps everything in place, holding it together.

The context we talk about when we're constructing The Ultimate Business Owner Plan is: 1. Tax Minimization; 2. Asset Protection; 3. Income Protection. Let's take a look at each.

Tax Minimization...

There is a difference between tax minimization and tax evasion. Tax evasion means jail. Tax minimization means legally taking advantage of ways we can save money on taxes. We focus on tax minimization because there is no reason why someone should pay more taxes than need be. There are three types of taxes we focus on: 1. Income taxes; 2. Estate or inheritance taxes; 3. Capital gains taxes. We look to minimize all three of these as much as the law allows.

The Threats Every Business Owner Needs to Be Aware of...

The next part of the context is Asset Protection. A business owner may or may not be aware that there is a bulls eye painted on his or her back. The outside world is aiming for that bulls eye and the assets the business owner has worked so hard to attain. There are lots of ways someone's assets can be attacked and The Ultimate Business Owner Plan prevents someone's life from getting destroyed because of frivolous lawsuits or unfortunate accidents.

We quarterback the process of building a huge wall between the business owner's assets and the outside world. We work with skilled asset protection attorneys all over the country who use legal ways designed to help the business owner protect the business and the family. There are dozens of ways this can be done. The best way is the one that fits with the business owner's goals and unique situation. There is no magic bullet or one-size-fits-all solution.

The last one, if you think of a pyramid and the foundation of the pyramid, this one actually is below the foundation. It is really the foundation of the foundation in my thinking. That's Income Protection. If we don't have income coming in, due to illness or an accident, everything else falls apart. Everything else disappears. You're going to have to sell your business. You're going to have to sell your assets. You're going to have liquidate things if you don't have income coming in to just be able to pay basic lifestyle expenses. Ensuring we've got income coming in, under any circumstance is a critical part of the process and context.

Susan: These three elements, income protection, tax minimization, and asset protection are the jar that you described earlier?

Steve: Yes.

Susan: Every business owner needs to be aware of these issues because all three of them, if they're not handled, are a threat to the business owner?

Steve: Yes. That's exactly right.

Susan: Tie this in for me, Steve, back to your original point of creating the life you want. How is this tied in to our vision for our life goals we articulated in the exercise earlier?

Steve: I have a client who's now in his 80s but sold his business for mid-eight figures a few years ago. He could have sold it for much more years before. But he was confident his life was about work.

I asked him more than a decade ago, "Why won't you accept these amazing offers to sell your business?" He looked me square in the eye and said, "What would I do?" He had no vision of life after owning his business. It was his identity.

Fast forward a couple of years. He had an unfortunate lawsuit which came up. He did all he could to defend himself and the lawsuit was pretty frivolous, but that is not how a jury saw it. He lost a lot of money. It took a big bite out of his business, and really took him on a detour to have to rebuild from that. It took him years to get back to the point that he could sell his business, albeit for less.

The happy ending is that he has a great life now. He travels extensively. He is active with his grandkids. He works out daily. He loves his life and still dabbles in investing in others' businesses.

But how much sooner could that have begun? How much time—about 10 years actually—did he miss enjoying life because he didn't: 1. Have a plan of the life he really wanted to live and; 2. Have a great asset protection plan in place.

That's the tie in between our financial structure...and our lives. That's what is possible with The Ultimate Business Owner Plan.

Susan: Right, someone may be at risk and they don't even realize it.

Steve: Exactly. We work with people to plug the holes they know are there, and maybe point out and plug some holes that they don't even realize are causing leaks in their boat.

Susan: Because as you pointed out at the beginning, we get so caught up in the running of the business, we never stop to assess things at the

20,000-foot level and find out I am at more risk than I need to be?

Steve: No one likes this conversation to be honest. It's not sexy to talk about my asset protection plan at the cocktail party. However if you want to achieve the best life that you can, as you define it, in your terms, you've got to make sure you protect what you've got, and keep yourself on that path and not let the outside world derail you. Life still happens. I am not saying that we can protect against every sort of calamity, but we certainly can shore up against most everything that happens.

Susan: To have a successful business and not have some of these elements in place, it's probably a false sense of security. We live in such a litigious country.

Steve: That's one side but there's even more pervasive ones. Let's think back to 2008. I was having a conversation with a very successful business owner recently, and he was talking about the faulty thinking that he had in the past. He didn't really plan because he always figured he could sell more. Through the '90s and early part of the 2000's up until 2008, if he wanted a bigger house or more income for something, he just had to figure out how to sell more.

If he wanted to expand his business, he just had to work harder somewhere. He could always find a way to create more income and therefore more profit. I think a lot of business owners were in that place. It's also why so many spent frivolously. So many business owners had bloated budgets and bought expensive baubles that were not necessary because they weren't concerned. Money was easy to manifest.

Suddenly boom, 2008 hits and it's like a two by four across the face. Now, we find it very difficult to sell at all, let alone sell as much as we want or make as much money as we made in the past. Maybe this didn't happen to everybody but certainly, many business owners found themselves in terrible situations.

I had a general contracting business as a client, 60-year-old business, third generation in fact. In 2007, they did $135 million of revenue. In 2008, things started to slow down and they did $105 million of revenue. Pretty big $30 million drop, wouldn't you say? In 2009, they did $15 million dollars of business. In 2010 they were out of business. At one time, they had 950 employees and then three years later, gone, out of business. A 60-year business closed. Hundreds of jobs lost and families in trouble.

What makes me sad is that could have been prevented. Planning could have prevented that business failure. It can't prevent what happens in the economy, but it can affect how you are protected against the effects of economic downturn. But most didn't plan because: 1. They were too busy worrying about business problems of today and; 2. They had a mindset of "That can never happen to us."

Susan: I'm guessing they didn't have any kind of income protection, correct?

Steve: They didn't have asset protection and they didn't have income protection in place.

Susan: To use your analogy, they put all their eggs in the grow category of their business, but they didn't stop and protect what they had.

Steve: That's right. They didn't and as a result they didn't get to enjoy. They were enjoying along the way but they're not enjoying things today, believe me.

Now these guys are in their late 60s and it's not exactly easy to pick up and rebuild.

Susan: In a blink of an eye, just a couple of years, the entire future changed and not for the better.

Steve: I have another client who has a distribution business and sells primarily for one manufacturer. He hit a hundred million dollar sales mark with that manufacturer. As a result, they sent him a bonus for $2 million near the end of November a few years ago. He called me after Thanksgiving and said, "I'm getting this great bonus but I don't want to have to pay taxes on all this money. What do I do?"

We were able to work with him to develop a plan that not only reduced his tax obligation, but created a risk management tool called a captive insurance company. Section 831(b) of the IRS code allows businesses like his to establish insurance companies to insure against legitimate risks of the business. It is a bit complicated and a lot of rules and regulations must be followed—it must be a legitimate insurance company and risks must be quantified in a sophisticated actuarial report. However under Section 831(b) a captive insurance company can have premium income of up to $1,200,000 without paying taxes on that premium. The business receives a tax deduction for the legitimate premium that it pays to the captive insurance company the owner has established. It's a very effective risk management tool that also has tax benefits.

Also, the money inside the captive insurance company is asset protected. Just like any insurance company, if the business has a claim arise that could be covered under the insurance policies that captive issues to the business, the owner can decide if he chooses to file a claim and take money out of the captive or just pay for the loss out of cash flow.

Lastly, we can have the captive owned outside of the owner's estate so that this can assist in estate tax planning also.

So this strategy can solve several issues the owner has and jump start his Ultimate Business Owner Plan.

The Building Blocks of The Ultimate Business Owner Plan...

Susan: I would imagine yes. Where do you go next with this Steve?

Steve: The specific building blocks of the pyramid of The Ultimate Business Owner Plan is where we go next. The most important part of any pyramid are the cornerstones and then the third piece of the foundation. So we focus on making sure business owners have a solid foundation built. You would be surprised how many don't.

There Are Many Reasons to Have an Exit Plan in Place...

Let's talk about the first cornerstone which is the Exit Plan. It sounds counterintuitive to say, "I should know how I am going to exit my business when I'm still working on building my business or perhaps, I'm even just starting my business". Stephen Covey talks about "begin with the end in mind."

If your business is going to be your biggest asset and your best asset – which for most business owners, it is – you've got to figure out what you're going to do with that asset to achieve your life goals. I'm not just talking about selling. How you exit the business might be to pass it on to your children or a key employee.

It might be important to you that this business becomes a legacy and goes on for multiple generations. If that's the case, it's important to know that and then to work towards that end as soon as possible. If that is my goal, I am going to build a business very differently and put in very different systems and strategies than if I am trying to sell out to the highest bidder at some time in the future.

There's nothing wrong with that strategy. The point is whichever one of those is your strategy or any other potential strategy that you have, it's best to begin with that in mind. It's critical you get clear on what your ideal way to get out of the business is and then work towards that end because monetizing the business is going to be the single biggest financial event of almost any business owner's life.

That's if you get there. Remember, most businesses don't even succeed past five years. We're really talking about adolescent, mature businesses here that have the ability to do that. For the startup however, you probably have a much greater chance of success in getting to that point if you begin with that end in mind rather than just being a victim of circumstances and seeing whatever happens and hope you have a business worth something down the road.

Susan: Are you saying Steve, depending on which exit strategy they choose you may want to structure a different kind of business for them depending on how they want to get out of the business?

Steve: Let's put it this way. If I want to pass my business on to my children, I am going to find a way to bring my children into the business in a way that doesn't upset my current employees, that teaches them what they need to learn not only to do whatever job they're doing but to be the eventual owner of that business, and have the leadership skills to be able to run the company. I would put together a process that ultimately positions them to naturally, gracefully step into taking over the business when it's time for me to exit.

That's very different than if I am trying to build a business to sell to a multinational corporation for a large multiple of earnings at some point in the future, and be off to Tahiti, never to be heard from again.

Susan: I see. Those are two very, different...

Steve: Two very different strategies yes, and then in the day-to-day operations, let alone, year-to-year, and decade-to-decade structures, and thought processes, and actions that would be undertaken inside of the business would be very different.

It's whatever it is that the business owner envisions. If I could do anything, this is what I would want to have happen. Feel free to dream. Dream big. What is it that I would want to have happen when I exit my business? Then, let's work backwards and say, how would you have to build your business to make that a reality?

Again, that's not Steve talking, that's attributed to Michael Gerber, but it's an important message for business owners to hear. They don't hear it often enough, if at all.

Estate Planning...

Susan: Well said. What's the next cornerstone?

Steve: The next cornerstone is Estate Planning which is related yet different. The exit plan is about the business itself and your greatest asset. The estate plan looks at all of your assets and hopefully, you create lots of assets outside the business. Ultimately, the way to protect one's self against the downturn in business is to have plenty of assets that are outside the business that are not directly dependent on the business.

Too many business owners reinvest all their capital back into the business. They pay themselves little. They just put it all back in the business to try and grow the business. Well-intentioned but it is short sighted, which was the problem in 2008 for a lot of business owners. If you've plowed all your money back into the business for all these years, and now your business is gone in a heartbeat, now what? What if you had created structures of outside assets that you could draw upon during the tough times to be able to weather the downturn?

Estate planning looks at how to pass on those assets to the next generation, whom you want, when you want with an eye to minimize taxes, to make sure their wealth is passed down responsibly. What do I want to have happen with my assets and to whom do I want to benefit, and so forth.

That can be a very complicated process if you have a lot of assets. There are many professionals who do nothing but estate planning. There are lots of ways to make sure your assets end up where you want and minimize estate taxes, but the structures can be very complicated. Estate planning can be rather simple if you don't have many assets. For all, it can be difficult emotionally however because people have weird attitudes about money. Their identities and money are often linked or they have a hard time talking about money with their kids or the next generation. We all have old programs or as T. Harv Eker refers to them, the financial blueprints, that were created inside our brains from the experiences we have had regarding money as children and in our pasts. It's looking through not only how do I want to pass these assets on but really what is my relationship with money and what do I want it to be?

Susan: You need to have these in place because if you don't, then as you pointed out with the gentleman who lost everything from the downturn in 2008, he wouldn't be where he is today if he had the three cornerstones in place.

Steve: That was three brothers, not just one guy, but yes.

Susan: Really?

Steve: Their father had started the business. Three brothers were running it, and now their kids were working in the business, and all of those opportunities plus the 950 jobs that they have created were gone at one time.

Susan: Crazy.

Steve: I had another client who had an engineering firm and he lived well below his means. During the good times, he was making a lot of money, well in the seven figures every year. He lived on a $200,000 or $300,000 lifestyle, and he plowed a lot of money into a special trust he created. In addition to his business he had not only cash, he had income-producing real estate and he had securities.

Of course, all of it dropped in value when the economy tanked. His business dropped precipitously overnight. He told me a story of literally looking at himself in the mirror and saying, "Do I want to go small, and just have a small operation and make a living or do I wanted to tap into these assets that I've put away and rebuild this business and try and make it big again?"

He did the latter. He tapped into those assets. He lived off them for a little bit. But because he planned ahead he took some of what he set aside and risked it in building his business. He's now back up to where he did $12 million dollars in revenue again last year.

Susan: Very nice. An example of protecting his assets.

Steve: It really paid off for him. Having those outside assets really can make a big difference for you. You never know what life is going to throw you.

Essential Financial Planning...

Susan: Absolutely.

Steve: Getting back to the pyramid. Your financial protection plan is your basic financial planning. I hate to use the 'B' word, budget, but we need to look at those things for not only business but our lives. It is easy to spend without really thinking about what we're doing. We don't often stop and ask ourselves what role the things that we spend money on play towards our goals and life?

I'm not the guy that says be a penny pincher and be a coupon clipper or anything like that. Enjoy life today but do it in a way that still gives you room to put away money for the future. Go through the process of budgeting but make sure the proper insurance is in place. Having this day-to-day financial protection plan in place gives us a roadmap of how to operate with the income we do bring in.

Susan: Agreed. I see why budget is on the bottom of the pyramid. It's fundamental; every business owner has to have this in place.

Steve: It doesn't have to be a dirty word either. It just depends on how you choose to look at it. If you choose to look at it as a horrible, restrictive and awful process, that's your choice. Another way to look at it is that it's a road map that I choose to create to help me get the life I want and I've got to have some discipline in my life. There is no way that anyone can think they can live an undisciplined life and come out with a life they want.

You can't have cotton candy for breakfast, lunch, and dinner and come out with a life that you want. You've got to have some sort of discipline around the food you're eating. It's the same with money. Discipline is a tough thing. Will power is a tough thing. Structure is a tough thing. People's relationship to money and their financial blueprint from the past comes into play and so it can be something they immediately react to in a negative way but with the proper mindset, it can be empowering, and really, free someone to live the life they want which is the goal of The Ultimate Business Owner Plan.

Susan: I couldn't agree more. Some people may think budgeting is restrictive but it's actually a very freeing process.

Retirement Income Plan...

Steve: The next building block is their Retirement Income Plan. Having a clear picture of what retirement looks like, and more and more, I don't even use that word with people. Instead I use the word financial independence. When could you be financially independent? When could you be working by choice not out of necessity? What a freeing concept that is, that I'm working because I choose to and not because I have to.

To do that, I have to have a plan. What lifestyle do I want? How much money do I need to support the lifestyle that I want in today's dollars? If we take a factor of inflation into consideration, and inflation has averaged approximately 3% over the last many years, and we increase that income amount by the inflation factor, it tells us in the future how much income I'll need to have the same purchasing power as my lifestyle today.

For example, if I want to have a lifestyle of a $100,000, if inflation averages 3% over the next 24 years, I'll need $200,000 24 years from now to buy the same amount of stuff that $100,000 buys today. Then, another 24 years after that, it will be $400,000, and so on.

Then, we have to work back and ask, "How much assets would you have to have to generate that much income?" We go back to the estate plan and creating outside assets. We go back to the exit plan and hopefully, what the value of the business is, but we put this all into an overall plan of utilizing structures. One of the best things that the Federal Government has done for us is to create structures that assist us in saving for future financial independence and having tax breaks now or tax breaks in the future for doing so.

Putting all these tools together to be able to reach that goal is a beautiful process when it's done right because it gives us financial independence and allows us to work because we choose to and not because we have to.

Susan: That's very exciting Steve. I can see how everything works together as one cohesive strategy. Is the plan strictly for their business or is this for their personal use?

Steve: In my view, there is no difference between my business and my life. My business is part of my life. What I do as a financial advisor is to look at all the pieces somebody has and say how can we use these pieces to the best way? What other pieces do we need to add? How can we put these all together to create a finished puzzle that means financial independence?

Susan: Thank you for clarifying.

Key Employee Incentive/Retention Plan...

Steve: The next building block is one people don't think about, but if I'm going to build a successful business, I can't do all the work myself. I've got to leverage myself. The more that I leverage myself effectively, the more free I am from the business. The more value the business has now and in the future. The more that I can have the work of the business done by others, the more free I am. The more value my business has, no one is going to pay for a business that has no value without you there. If I am the best salesperson in the business, if I am the face of the business, if I handle all the problems, if it's all built around me, a future owner is not going to pay very much if I am not going to be there. It's not worth very much.

Likewise, what does my life look like on an ongoing basis? How can I go on vacation because nothing gets done if the business is built around me? I've got to leverage myself through employees. Some people look at employees as a negative thing but I see them as an incredibly positive thing. Some of my best relationships I've had in my life have been with my employees . They're great people and very supportive and completely dedicated to the business.

I've seen this with lots of my clients where they've just got amazing people who work with them. They may be employees but they work with them to really build this business and they leverage the business owner. Often times, they are much better at particular areas than the business owner is. Finding those people, retaining those people, and incenting those people is critical. The only way we can grow our business to be all it can be is by leveraging yourself through others.

We create plans I call key employee protection and incentive plans to do all those things: recruit, retain, reward, incent, and then, protect ourselves in case, God forbid, one of those key people dies or becomes disabled. This is a critical step towards having a business that can be all it can be.

Susan: Interesting that you include this in the planning process.

Steve: It is, but it's why it's not down at the bottom. As businesses mature, as I am moving towards this place of ultimately enjoying the value of my business, I've got key employees as a business owner. Any business owner is going to have these people. If you don't intentionally go about rewarding, retaining and incenting those people, protecting yourself against the loss of those people, your business is in jeopardy. It's part of the whole picture. It can't be overlooked.

Legacy Plan

The last aspect to The Ultimate Business Owner plan is the apex of the pyramid. Honestly, this is more important to some people than others. Leaving a legacy, leaving the world a better place, to me is a lofty goal whether it's through our children, the business which does great work that we leave behind, the charitable work that we leave, or the charitable bequests we make to causes we care about, or mentoring that we do with people. We all have time, treasure, and talent that we have to offer.

Having a plan of how I'm going to leave the world a better place either now or when I'm not here, I think is one of the highest callings we can have. It's not about your spirituality. It's a lofty goal and something to aspire to.

If that's not something that someone aspires to, fine. We don't have to work on that. To a lot of the really successful business owners I know their legacy is the most important goal.

Successful People Do What Unsuccessful Are Unwilling to Do...

Successful people do what unsuccessful people are unwilling to do. Successful people think differently than unsuccessful people. I think that it's not an accident that successful business owners often are very charitable or often want to leave a big legacy because they think about something bigger than themselves and something outside of themselves.

It attaches meaning to what they do so that when they're building their business, when they're working in their business, when they're going through this day-to-day grind, there is a greater purpose for what they are doing which makes that day-to-day grind much more enjoyable, which makes them do it much better, which makes them much more successful, which then leaves a bigger legacy.

Susan: This is a pretty comprehensive plan you're talking about here. There's a lot of moving parts - a lot of ways to engage with the business owner.

Steve: Yes, there can be.

Susan: Do you find business owners want to tackle one piece at a time or do they want to tackle the whole pyramid?

Steve: I'd say most business owners, when they really get it, want the whole thing. However, it's too much to bite off all in one chunk for most people. While we try to look holistically, we meet someone where they're at. We find out what their ultimate dreams and goals are. We suggest ways to get from point A, where they're at now, to point B, this future they envision. But then we prioritize what's most important, where do they want to get started and let's get to work on some of it because again, this is a journey and not a destination.

You can never be done with this work but you can get to work on a piece of it, and then another one, and then another one and so forth, and then go back and improve, start again from the beginning. It can be a lifelong process. It can be a lot of fun, too.

Susan: Sound like it's very rewarding for you.

Steve: I love what I do. I love working with successful entrepreneurs who get this and are engaged in this process, and want to make a difference, and care. My ideal client is a business owner who cares about his or her employees, and cares about the community, and cares about their family, and cares about the future and is coachable. That's the type of person that I work best with and I find a lot of entrepreneurs are like that. It's a tremendously rewarding process to work with them on creating a business that supports their life in the highest possible way.

Here's Exactly How to Get Your Ultimate Business Owner Plan Started...

Susan: Can you describe how the process works?

Steve: There are two places to engage. It's really about figuring out where you're at and where you want to go and then how you want to get there. The best way is we have a conversation and we start using the tools on the pyramid. We have laid out tools for each step in the process. This is not a happenstance or make it up as we go. I've been doing this for more than a quarter century. I've used those experiences and taking bits and pieces as I've learned from some of the greatest business minds that are out there. I won't take credit for very many original thoughts but I'll take credit for exposing myself to great thinking by others, and taking pieces of their tools, and putting it into a process that can lead a business owner to achieve the life they dream.

It all starts with a conversation. We start working through the tools. If the exit plan and getting clear on what that looks like is a concept that resonates with somebody, that's a great place to start for a business owner. We have a simple 20-question survey that someone can take called the Business Exit Readiness Index Report. They answer ten questions about how financially ready they are to exit their business, and ten questions about how mentally ready they are to exit their business.

It creates a very elegant report that can be a point of discussion and give them some feedback and some information about where they're at. You can start the process of creating The Ultimate Business Owner

Plan on any of the cornerstones depending on where the client is. It's not about me telling you what to do. It's about my business facilitating a process by which you are able to create your own Ultimate Business Owner Plan.

Susan: I love it. How can someone reach you Steve?

Steve: They can go to www.FinancialSolutions4Business.com and it will be apparent how to get started down either of those paths.

Susan: This is exciting, Steve, because you've tied it back to where the business owner really does want to go? What do they want in life? Let's use their business as a tool to get them there, rather than just being the tail to the dog.

Steve: Yes, well it's a process that's been successful for over 25 years and it's really life changing for my clients. Thanks Susan for facilitating this discussion.

Susan: Thanks Steve for sharing this with us today.

Author Bio

Steve Beatty stepped into the financial advising world in 1989. His expertise is working alongside owners of closely held businesses for almost 20 years. Since 1993, Steve has been a member of the esteemed Million Dollar Roundtable and has qualified for the Top of the Table since 2004, a distinction of only the top 0.2% of financial advisors worldwide.

Strategic tax planning, wealth management, exit and estate planning are all areas that Steve specializes in and has worked in extensively. He earned his Political Science degree from the University of California-San Diego. Steve was one of the first graduates of the 401(k) Coach Program, a national program from prominent 401(k) advisors.

At age 16, Steve started as a sportswriter for the Colorado Springs Gazette-Telegraph, San Diego Union and Los Angeles Times. During his junior year of college, he met his wife Hilde on an exchange program to Bergen, Norway. They were married in 1989 and live in Las Vegas, Nevada with their three children. Steve enjoys golf and racquetball.

Professional Achievements

- Million Dollar Roundtable Member since 1993
  The Premier Association for Financial Professionals®
    -Top of the Table Member since 2004
    -Court of the Table Member since 2002
- Wealthy 100
    -Member and Founder of Las Vegas chapter
- Top 40 Under 40
    -In Business Las Vegas

Community Service

- Faith Lutheran Junior and Senior High Business Advisory Council
    -Executive Board Member
- Girls Youth Softball Coach
- Boys Youth Baseball Coach

Here Is How to Get Your Ultimate Business Owner Plan Designed and in Place...

You've created a successful business. The tough part is knowing what are the right financial strategies to protect what you've built and to ensure you'll be able to enjoy yourself along the way and at retirement. Even harder is knowing what are the right strategies for you and your unique goals and situation.

That's where we come in. We help people just like you structure your Ultimate Business Plan that gives you the peace of mind and feeling of accomplishment you've been craving.

Step 1: We invest 45 minutes understanding where you are and where you want to go with your life and your business. This step is critical and often overlooked.

Step 2: We help you discover the key strategies used to minimize your taxes, protect your business and your loved ones from threats and find out where you may not be leveraging the greatest asset you will ever own, YOUR BUSINESS, to provide maximum benefits for you now and in the future.

Step 3: Together we design your Ultimate Business Owner Plan. We layout our step-by-step process for you to get what most business owners are not aware of: The power of a comprehensive financial strategy like this. We've been working with high income, high net worth business owners for more than 25 years to develop this process so you can focus on what's important to you--running your business and spending time doing what you love with the people you care about.

If you'd like us to help, just send an email to sbeatty@financialsolutions4business.com or visit: www.FinancialSolutions4Business.com to get started right away and we will take it from there.